Mike Slaughter

with Karen Perry Smith

REVOLUTIONARY KINGDOM

Following the Rebel Jesus

Leader Guide

by Alex Joyner

Abingdon Press / Nashville

Revolutionary Kingdom:
Following the Rebel Jesus
Leader Guide

Copyright © 2019 Abingdon Press
All rights reserved.

ISBN 978-1-5018-8728-4
ISBN 978-1-5018-8729-1 ebook

19 20 21 22 23 24 25 26 27 28 — 10 9 8 7 6 5 4 3 2 1
MANUFACTURED IN THE UNITED STATES OF AMERICA

CONTENTS

TO THE LEADER

Congratulations! As the leader of this study, you have a great opportunity to go deeper into this study of the revolutionary nature of the kingdom of God. It's often said that the best way to have a deep learning experience is to be a leader or teacher. You get to do that with a group of other explorers. And in addition to the study book you are using, you also have this leader guide, which will give the resources you need for six powerful learning sessions.

This leader guide is designed to be used with Mike Slaughter's book, *Revolutionary Kingdom: Following the Rebel Jesus.* Mike Slaughter is pastor emeritus and global ambassador for Ginghamsburg Church, a United Methodist congregation in Tipp City, Ohio, that has grown to four campuses. Mike is passionate about creating vibrant, vital churches that reflect the diversity of the communities they serve. He is also committed to developing new church leaders who get the vision of God's revolutionary kingdom.

In this book, Mike builds on his previous book, *Renegade Gospel: Rebel Jesus,* to help followers of Jesus strengthen their commitment to Christ. (It is not necessary to have read *Renegade Gospel* in order to use and benefit from *Revolutionary Kingdom.*) Slaughter believes that a key part of Christian discipleship is embracing a kingdom-of-God worldview. This book challenges readers to let Jesus' Kingdom message lead us to looking at our current worldview in new ways. Along the way Mike tackles relevant, timely issues in the world from a Kingdom perspective and provides example of a missional lifestyle.

This leader guide provides you with the resources you need to lead your group. In fact, you probably have *more* material than you need. So, you can choose from the options in the "Learning Together" sections to fit the time you have for your group meetings.

There are six sessions in this study, and it makes use of the following components:

- Mike Slaughter's book *Revolutionary Kingdom: Following the Rebel Jesus,*
- the DVD that accompanies the study, and
- this Leader Guide.

Participants in the study should plan on bringing Bibles and the *Revolutionary Kingdom* study book to each session. If possible, notify those interested in the study in advance of the first session. Make arrangements for them to get copies of the book so they can read the introduction and chapter 1 before the first group meeting.

Using This Guide with Your Group

The format for a typical session is provided below. It is designed to give you options and flexibility in planning your sessions with your group. You will want to develop your sessions with your group in mind. Choose any or all of the activities. Adapt. Reorder. Rearrange. Innovate. This is the raw material for your lesson planning.

The session plans in this leader guide are designed to be completed in a session of about 60 to 90 minutes in length, but you can use fewer activities to reduce the time to as little as 45 minutes. Depending on which activities you select, there may be special preparation needed. The leader is alerted in the session plan about the advance preparation that is needed.

Session Format

Planning the Session

Session Goals
Scriptural Foundation
Special Preparation

Getting Started

Opening Activity
Opening Prayer

Learning Together

Video Study and Discussion
Book and Bible Study and Discussion

Wrapping Up

Closing Activity
Closing Prayer

Optional Element

Journaling

Journaling is a wonderful way to encourage more individual reflection and more extensive interaction outside the group sessions. You can promote the use of a journal by using one of your own as part of your preparation and class time. Group members can use any sort of book they would like for journaling, from a composition book to a bound, blank journal to a set of loose-leaf paper. Encourage those who take on this option to use the journal for reflecting on the reading, writing questions for future learning, and considering commitments they might make for their own spiritual growth. Some of the exercises suggested in the session plans can be done in the journal during class.

Helpful Hints

Preparing for the Session

1. Pray. You are on an important journey. Pray for God's guidance as you discern and lead. Pray, as well, for the members of your group.

2. Before each session, familiarize yourself with the content. Read the book chapter again.

3. Depending on the length of time you have available for group meetings, you may or may not have time to do all the activities. Select the activities in advance that will work for your group time and interests.

4. Choose the session elements you will use during the group session, including the specific discussion questions you plan to cover. Be prepared, however, to adjust the session as group members interact and as questions arise.

5. Prepare the room where the group will meet so that the space will enhance the learning process. Ideally, group members should be seated around a table or in a circle or semicircle so that all can see each other. Moveable chairs are best because the group will sometimes be forming pairs or small groups for discussion. Special seating arrangements for some sessions are also suggested in the planning notes.

6. Bring a supply of Bibles for those who forget to bring their own.

7. For most sessions you will also need a whiteboard and markers, or an easel with large sheets of paper and markers. You will also see suggestions for preparing large sheets of paper before the sessions.

Shaping the Learning Environment

- Begin and end on time.
- Create a climate of openness, encouraging group members to participate as they feel comfortable.
- Remember that some people will jump right in with answers and comments, while others need time to process what is being discussed.
- If you notice that some group members seem never to be able to enter the conversation, ask them if they have thoughts to share. Give everyone a chance to talk, but keep the conversation moving. Moderate to prevent a few individuals from doing all the talking.

- Communicate the importance of group discussions and group exercises.
- If no one answers at first during discussions, do not be afraid of silence. Count silently to ten, then say something such as, "Would anyone like to go first?" If no one responds, venture an answer yourself and ask for comments.
- Model openness as you share with the group. Group members will follow your example. If you limit your sharing to a surface level, others will follow suit.
- Encourage multiple answers or responses before moving on.
- To help continue a discussion and give it greater depth, ask, "Why?" or "Why do you believe that?" or "Can you say more about that?"
- Affirm others' responses with comments such as "Great" or "Thanks" or "Good insight," especially if it's the first time someone has spoken during the group session.
- Monitor your own contributions. If you are doing most of the talking, back off so that you do not train the group to listen rather than speak up.
- Remember that you do not have all the answers. Your job is to keep the discussion going and encourage participation.

Managing the Session

- Honor the time schedule. If a session is running longer than expected, get consensus from the group before continuing beyond the agreed-upon ending time.
- Involve group members in various aspects of the group session, such as saying prayers or reading the Scripture.
- Note that the session guides sometimes call for breaking into smaller groups or pairs. This gives everyone a chance to speak and participate fully. Mix up the groups; don't let the same people pair up for every activity.
- As always in discussions that may involve personal sharing, confidentiality is essential. Group members should never pass along stories that have been shared in the group. Remind the group

members at each session: confidentiality is crucial to the success of this study.

A Special Note

Revolutionary Kingdom is a bold book that highlights issues that have the potential to spark heated debate. It is important to remind group members frequently that this study is designed to look at issues that cause political conflict in other settings through the eyes of Jesus' message of the kingdom of God. Encourage the group to set aside political agendas in order to hear what Mike Slaughter is saying, to hear what each other is saying, and to hear what God is saying. Encourage listening and openness. If conversations become tense, pause, breathe, and pray. Do not allow conversation of one issue to dominate sessions and keep you from moving through the lesson plan.

Session 1

THE GOSPEL OF THE KINGDOM OF GOD

Planning the Session

Session Goals

As a result of conversations and activities connected with this session, group members should begin to

- understand the focus of Mike Slaughter's book as an exploration of what it means for disciples of Jesus Christ to embrace a kingdom-of-God worldview;
- examine biblical passages that illustrate the gospel of the kingdom of God and its alternative politic;
- identify how current social issues look through the lens of the Kingdom and how Christians can develop practices of social holiness;
- delineate the differences between a nationalistic identity and the kingdom of God as an alternative society governed by Christ.

Scriptural Foundation

> "Now is the time! Here comes God's kingdom! Change your hearts and lives, and trust this good news!"
>
> *(Mark 1:15)*

Special Preparation

- Prepare the room with seating arranged in a circle so that everyone will be able to see each other.
- Create a small worship space in the center of the circle with visual reminders of God's presence. For this session, that could include a candle, an open Bible, and a cross.
- If this is a new group or you have new members for this study, have nametags available as well as pens and markers.
- Have available paper, pens, pencils, markers, and other drawing materials.
- Also have available Bibles for those who may not have brought one. Encourage participants to bring a Bible for future sessions.
- Get two large sheets of posterboard and cut each sheet into four pieces. Have available masking tape or some other means to affix the posterboard to the wall during the exercise "Study Scripture Together."
- Prepare a large sheet of paper with the words "Revolutionary Kingdom" written across the top. Leave plenty of space beneath each word for the exercise in the opening activity. Post the sheet in a visible place in your meeting space.
- Post another large sheet of paper in a visible space as well.
- Watch the video segment for Session 1 prior to the session. Prepare a question or two to be used for discussion. Make sure you have a means to show the video to the group.
- Have a timer available for the exercise "Examine the State of the Church."

Getting Started

Opening Activity

As participants arrive, greet them and invite them into a circle of chairs. If it is a newly formed group, have each person write his or her name on a nametag and put it on. Begin the session with brief introductions. As a prompt, encourage group members to share something that makes them uncomfortable that they put up with for a larger purpose. For instance, a long plane flight may be uncomfortable but if a reunion with someone we love is on the other end, we tolerate the discomfort.

After this exercise, thank the group for sharing, then say the following:

- *In this study, Mike Slaughter will be asking us to step out of our places of comfort in order to become stronger disciples of Jesus. The book we are reading together challenges us to see the world through the lens of the kingdom of God, which Jesus talked about a lot. This group should be a safe place to share our discomfort and our struggles with honesty and openness to one another. Let's start by talking about the title of the book, which might make us uncomfortable right away!*

Direct the group's attention to the large sheet of paper that you posted in a visible spot before the session began titled "Revolutionary Kingdom." Begin by asking the group members to call out associations that they have with the word *Revolutionary*. What is exciting about it? What is unsettling? Revolutions can bring needed change, but they can also bring chaos. As persons respond, write their responses on the sheet under the word *Revolutionary*.

Now do the same with the word *Kingdom*. What is attractive about the idea of kingdoms? What is off-putting? Kingdoms establish order but they can be oppressive. Write responses under the word *Kingdom*.

After allowing some time for this exercise, say:

- *Thanks for beginning this journey with your willingness to share both the excitement and discomfort of seeking Jesus' revolutionary kingdom. We'll have many more opportunities to share in the sessions ahead. I'm glad we're on the journey together.*

Opening Prayer

Pray together using the following prayer or one of your own:

Christ of the narrow gate, you call us out of our places of comfort to discover new life with you. Thank you for calling us together for this time of study and growth. Keep us open to one another and to you. Amen.

Learning Together

Video Study and Discussion

Play the video and ask the group for reactions to it. Ask a question or two that you prepared from viewing the video before the session.

Book and Bible Study and Discussion

What Does the Kingdom of God Look Like?

Say to the group:

- *In the first chapter of the book, Mike Slaughter talks about how the Jesus Movement of the late '60s and early '70s gave him an early picture of what the kingdom of God might look like. What were some of the social concerns that Mike was involved in as result of his time in the Campus Christian fellowship?*

Give the group the page number in the study book where Mike talks about this experience. Some of the possible answers are: environmental protection, responses to the Vietnam War, civil rights, and bringing good news to the poor. Ask:

- *How did this experience change Mike's understanding of what it means to be a follower of Jesus?*

Allow group members to respond.

Now invite the group to turn in their Bibles to Acts 2:42-47. Have a volunteer read the passage aloud while others follow along in their Bibles. Ask:

- *What were the practices of the early Christian community described here? How might these practices have made them stand out in the larger society? What feels uncomfortable about this vision of Christian community to you? How was God blessing this community?*

Write the words "Alternative Politic of the Kingdom of God" on a clean sheet of paper posted in a visible location in your meeting space.

Say to the group:

- *Mike Slaughter says that his Campus Christian fellowship saw itself as an alternative politic to the politics of the world. He says this alternative politic of the kingdom of God lives in prophetic tension with the world.*

Ask:

- *If we lived out the politics of the kingdom of God, where would we find ourselves in tension with the world?*

Write responses on the paper.

Explore What It Means That Christ Will Come Again

Say to the group:

- *One of the affirmations of the Christian faith is that Christ has died, Christ is risen, and Christ will come again.*

Ask:

- *What visual images do you have in your mind of Christ's return?*

Assure the group that you are not looking for a "right" answer but for the ways that we have envisioned Christ's return based on our training in the Christian faith.

Have a participant read aloud the section of chapter 1 in which the author talks about N. T. Wright's understanding of God's judgment. Provide the page reference so that group members can follow along. Ask:

- *How does N. T. Wright's idea of God's return to reign differ from images you have had of what Christ's return means? How can* judgment *have a positive meaning?*

Now have someone read the paragraph that includes the quote from Louis Evely. Say:

- *Louis Evely says that "the paradox of our time is that those who believe in God do not believe in the salvation of the world, and those who believe in the future of the world do not believe in God."*

Ask:

- *What do you think Evely means by this? How does the belief that God loves the world change the way we think about God's judgment of the world?*

Study Scripture Together

Divide into small groups of three or four people. Assign each group two of the following Scriptures that Mike Slaughter references in chapter 1 of the study book:

- Leviticus 19:33-34
- Deuteronomy 27:19
- Micah 6:8
- Amos 8:4-6
- Isaiah 1:17
- Zechariah 7:9
- Deuteronomy 16:20
- Proverbs 29:7

Distribute pieces of posterboard and markers to each small group. Say:

- *In chapter 1, Mike Slaughter lists these passages as places where biblical writers tell us what God desires to establish justice. Read the passages you have been assigned from the Bible. See if the verses around those assigned give you more insight into what the passage is saying. Paraphrase the passage in your own words and write your paraphrase on the posterboard you have been given. Consider what it would mean in our society today if we took this passage seriously.*

Give the small groups some time to work and then call them back together. Invite each group to present its paraphrase along with some of the implications the group members discussed about how we might respond to the passage today. Affix each piece of posterboard to the wall in a visible part of your meeting space. Ask:

- *How do these passages help us understand the social implications of the gospel of the kingdom of God? How is our community of faith involved in the issues raised here?*

Examine the State of the Church

Read, or have someone else read, Mike's story about the church he visited in Boston in chapter 1 of the study book. Say to the group:

- *Mike Slaughter says that he often has to fight his own cynicism about church.*

Ask:

- *What does Mike's story reveal about the state of some churches these days? What did Mike experience among the people who met in the basement of the Boston church?*

Now invite the group members to pair up with someone else in the group. Ask them to identify which of the two will be a speaker and which will be a listener. Tell the persons identified as speakers that they will have one minute in which to share a time when they felt disengaged from the institutional church and what caused that feeling. Instruct the listener that her or his job is simply to listen. Set a timer and give the speaker one minute to share. After one minute have the partners switch roles and have the new speaker tell his or her experience of disengagement.

Next, have everyone find a new partner and do the exercise again, this time by reflecting on a time when the group members felt very engaged with the church. What was going on? How did that experience help them feel connected to God and others? Once again, time the exercise.

Bring everyone back to the large group and ask:

- *What did you learn in hearing these stories? How did the voices and experiences of people outside the church enter your stories? What messages do these stories have for your community of faith?*

Discuss Nationalism and Citizenship in the Kingdom of God

Read, or have someone else read, the first three paragraphs in the section of chapter 1 titled "Misplaced Allegiance—The Flag or the Cross." Ask the group:

- *What is the problem with nationalism from the perspective of the kingdom of God? What alternative responses might we have to "outsiders" in need if we are responding as people whose citizenship is in heaven?*

Say to the group:

- *Mike Slaughter says that the kingdom of God always lives in tension with the nation-state.*

Ask:

- *What biblical passages does he use to illustrate this?*

Say:

- *Mike says that the prominence of the American flag in so many American Christian churches is a challenge to the Christian belief that Jesus is our ultimate authority.*

Ask:

- *Are there American flags in our church or on our property? Where are they? What does their placement say about how we view our allegiance to the nation in relation to our allegiance to Christ?*

Read aloud the paragraph in chapter 1 of the study book in which Mike Slaughter shares the story of a young Mississippi pastor who confronted the presence of the American flag and pledges to the flag in her congregation. Ask:

- *How is this an area of discussion in our community of faith? If we were to confront it here, how would we do it? How would we react to a pastoral leader who differed with our understanding?*

Wrapping Up

Closing Activity

Plan to Put On Your Kingdom Lenses

Invite group members to choose a time each day in the coming week to "put on their Kingdom lenses." Ask them to choose a minute of the day during which they will pause and ask themselves:

- *How does the world around me look through the lens of the kingdom of God? How can I respond to a situation I see here as a citizen of that Kingdom?*

Ask them to write down the time they have chosen. Encourage them to set an alarm on their phone or watch so they will remember to pause at that moment. Perhaps they might also choose a pair of sunglasses to put on during that minute as a physical expression of the alternative lenses they are trying to use.

Tell the group that you will ask them to share their experiences at the beginning of the next session.

Closing Prayer

Remind the group that Mike Slaughter talks about the Lord's Prayer as part of this chapter as an example of how Jesus saw God already at work bringing heaven to earth. Pray the Lord's Prayer together as your closing act of worship.

Session 2

THE COUNTERCULTURE KINGDOM COMMUNITY

Planning the Session

Session Goals

As a result of conversations and activities connected with this session, group members should begin to

- understand the biblical history of God's people as a called-out group living in covenant relationship with God for the purpose of service to the world;
- consider the gifts they have been given for ministry in the body of Christ and their commitment to following Christ;
- examine the way of love as one of the distinctive features of God's counterculture Kingdom;
- explore how our words and actions can make us receptive to God's work in us and can reveal our character.

Scriptural Foundation

You are a chosen race, a royal priesthood, a holy nation, a people who are God's own possession. You have become this people so that you may speak of the wonderful acts of the one who called you out of darkness into his amazing light. Once you weren't a people, but now you are God's people. Once you hadn't received mercy, but now you have received mercy.

(1 Peter 2:9-10)

Special Preparation

- Prepare the room with seating arranged in a circle so that everyone will be able to see each other.
- Create a small worship space in the center of the circle with visual reminders of God's presence. For this session that could include some stones, a cross, and seeds.
- Have available paper, pens, pencils, and other drawing materials. Also have sticky notes available for the activity in "Do an Open Source Exercise on the Gifts of the Community."
- Also have available Bibles for those who may not have brought one.
- Watch the video segment for Session 2 prior to the session. Prepare a question or two to be used for discussion. Make sure you have a means to show the video to the group.
- Post a large sheet of paper in a visible location in your meeting space for the exercise titled "Review the History of the Called-Out People."
- Post another large sheet of paper for exercise titled "Consider Our Words and Character."

Getting Started

Opening Activity

Tell Uniform Stories

Ask participants to recall a time when they wore a uniform. Possible scenarios might include service in the military, working in a restaurant, playing on a sports team, or participating in scouting. Invite the participants to turn to a neighbor and share how they felt while wearing the uniform. Ask them to consider these questions: *How did the uniform make you feel part of a team? What, if anything, made you feel uncomfortable? Why?*

After some time of sharing in pairs, come back together as a large group. Say:

- *Our stories of "life in uniform" give us a sense of what it means to be identified as part of a team. In chapter 2 of the study book, Mike Slaughter talks about how God has claimed us to be identified as a called-out people.*

Ask:

- *Since we don't wear uniforms, what are the identifying marks of Christians?*

Share Experiences with the Kingdom Lenses

Invite volunteers to share experiences they had in doing the daily exercise of "putting on their Kingdom lenses" (as described in the closing activity for Session 1). How did they see the world differently? What situations did they see in new ways?

Opening Prayer

Offer the following prayer or one of your own:

God of Abraham and Sarah, Moses and Miriam,
You have always been calling people to new adventures
*   and journeys they did not always want to undertake.*
We want to live as citizens of your counterculture Kingdom.
We want to understand with greater depth the ways you work in the world.
We want to be agents of your grace and mercy in this land.
Bless our time together and give us glimpses of adventures up ahead.
In the name of Jesus, the Way, we pray. Amen.

Learning Together

Video Study and Discussion

Play the video and ask the group for reactions to it. Ask a question or two that you prepared from viewing the video before the session.

Book and Bible Study and Discussion

Study Scripture Together

Invite the group to turn in their Bibles to 1 Peter 2:9-10. Say to the group:

- *This passage was written to an early Christian community that needed to be reminded of its identity in a world that challenged that identity. As we read this passage, imagine that you are Christians in those early days of the church when you would have been seen as a strange minority group in the culture.*

Have a volunteer read the passage aloud. Then ask:

- *How would you summarize the message of these verses to those early Christians?*

Now say:

- *We are going to read the passage a second time. This time, listen for what God might be saying to Christians living in our times.*

Ask a different volunteer to read through the passage this second time, perhaps in a different translation. Then ask:

- *What does it mean for us to be a "set-apart people" in our times? What are we called to do?*

Review the History of the Called-Out People

Divide into four small groups for this exercise. Assign one of the following stories from the opening section of chapter 2 to each of the groups:

1. Abraham
2. Moses
3. Israel
4. Jesus with the mother of two disciples

Say to the groups:

- *In the opening section of chapter 2, Mike Slaughter shares with us moments from the history of God's people that reveal what God's kingdom looks like. Find the paragraph (or paragraphs) related to the story you have been assigned and read them aloud in your small group. Then ask: What does this story show us about how God's kingdom works?*

Give the small groups some time to work. Then bring the whole group back together. Ask each group to report back on their discussion. As they share learnings, write these on a large sheet of paper that you have posted in a visible location in your meeting space. Say to the group:

- *Mike Slaughter says that the community of the church is supposed to be a visible expression of God's kingdom. If these qualities we have listed are part of the ethics of the Kingdom, how well does our church or community of faith express them?*

Now give group members a moment to reflect on their own discipleship. Invite participants to spend a minute in silence considering how they are feeling challenged to live out a commitment to God's kingdom. Perhaps it is a challenge to be more open, more sacrificial, or more oriented to service. Ask individuals to write down one thing that they could do in the coming week to be more available to do God's will in this area.

Do an Open Source Exercise on the Gifts of the Community

Pass around some sticky notes so that every participant has at least three. Ask each participant to write down on each of his or her sticky notes something that Jesus did in his earthly ministry. One example: "Jesus healed the sick."

After allowing some time for individuals to write, ask each person to read his or her notes to the group. If no one else has offered the example she or he has read, the individual should stick the note to a section of wall that you have designated for this exercise.

Once all the notes have been read aloud and placed on the wall, say to the group:

- *Mike Slaughter says that Kingdom people embody the work of Jesus in order to demonstrate God's grace and mercy to the world. Let's see what we can envision about living out Jesus' work as Jesus' hands and feet.*

Invite individuals who would like to lead a discussion about one of the examples on the sticky notes to go and remove that note, read it aloud, and stand with it in an open space in the room. Once two or three individuals have done this and are standing in different places in the room, invite everyone to choose one of the discussion groups and move to stand with that person. (If you have persons with physical disabilities that make it difficult or impossible for them to stand, you will need to accommodate this exercise accordingly.)

If there is one discussion leader who has no other participants, invite him or her to choose one of the other groups or to choose another sticky note and read it out, allowing persons to change groups as they wish.

Once everyone has chosen a group, say:

- *For the next five minutes, discuss what we, as people with unique gifts in the body of Christ, can do to continue this mission that Jesus began. For instance, if the example is that Jesus heals the sick, how can we continue that mission with our gifts?*

Ask the groups, if they are able, to have their discussion while they are standing up. Time them and after five minutes ask them to report back to the larger group. Are there ideas that could be implemented right away? visions that are worth further exploration? Write them down and take them to the pastoral and lay leaders in your community of faith.

Explore the Way of Love

Read aloud, or have a volunteer read, the three opening paragraphs of the section titled "The Way of Love" in chapter 2 of the study book. Ask:

- *According to Mike Slaughter, what is it about the church that seems to have turned off so many millennials and people like Gandhi?*

Ask participants to turn in their Bibles to Mark 12:28-31. Read the verses aloud. Ask:

- *What does Jesus say is the most important commandment? Why are many people outside the church not perceiving that Christians are living by this commandment?*

Read the section of chapter 2 in which Mike Slaughter talks about his experience in Adilla in East Darfur. Ask:

- *Where do you see love being expressed in this story? How does love overcome division?*

Say to the group:

- *Mike Slaughter talks about how the community of Jesus' disciples included a surprising diversity of personalities: Matthew the tax collector and Simon the Zealot, impulsive Peter and even Judas who betrayed Jesus.*

Invite group members to think about a type of person or even particular individuals that they find difficult to love. Now imagine that person being part of your most intimate community. Ask:

- *What challenges or fears would you have to overcome in order to show love toward that person? How does Jesus help us understand what it means to love our enemies? What would change about how the church is perceived if we did love our enemies?*

Consider Our Words and Character

Read aloud, or have someone else read, the first two paragraphs of the section titled "Hearing the Word of God" in chapter 2 of the study book. Say to the group:

- *Mike Slaughter uses the parable of the sower and the seed to emphasize our receptivity to God and God's intentions for the world. One of the indicators of our health as citizens of the kingdom of God is in the ways we use words.*

Invite the group to think of a time when they said or wrote something that they later regretted. Ask:

- *What were the circumstances that led you to say or write what you did? What considerations did you have about making amends? How did you follow up on them?*

Now ask group members to consider the environment of social media. Ask:

- *How do we respond when someone posts on social media with something that wounds or offends us? What could we do to contribute to a healthier discourse online?*

On a large sheet of paper posted in a visible location in your meeting space, write the words "Commandments for Kingdom Speaking." Now ask participants to offer commandments that would help us model Kingdom character in our communication. Write them on the sheet of paper. When you have finished the exercise, invite group members to take a picture of the sheet, if they have a smartphone. Alternatively, type up the commandments between sessions and have them available at your next gathering. Say to group members:

- *Our words reflect our character, and they have the power to hurt or heal.*

Ask:

- *What communities that you are involved in most need your healing words?*

Wrapping Up

Closing Activity

Read a Poem

Robert Frost's poem "The Road Not Taken" is included in chapter 2 as an example of making a commitment to follow a less-traveled path. Invite the group to read the poem in unison or go around the circle having group members read one line each.

Ask group members to reflect silently on the following questions, leaving some silence between each one:

- *How would you describe the tone of this poem?*
- *What sort of choices are you facing in your life?*
- *Which choice would better reflect your commitment to Christ?*

Bring a Bible Next Time

In preparation for the next session, invite group members to identify a Bible that has special meaning to them and bring it to the next session.

Closing Prayer

Offer the following prayer or one of your own:

Christ, who is the Way and Narrow Gate,
    we want to be receptive soil for your word.
We commit ourselves again to being
    members of your counterculture community
    and parts of your body in the world.
Let us take your road in every wood. Amen.

Session 3

REVOLUTIONARY AUTHORITY

Planning the Session

Session Goals

As a result of conversations and activities connected with this session, group members should begin to

- consider Protestant and Catholic models for dealing with differences in scriptural interpretation;
- explore insights that Scripture itself gives in answering key questions about the role and authority of Scripture for Christian faith and practice;
- appreciate the revolutionary authority represented by Jesus Christ, the Living Word, and the continuing presence and guidance of the Holy Spirit in the church;
- examine the source of Christian unity in the crucified Christ.

Scriptural Foundation

> *In the past, God spoke through the prophets to our ancestors in many times and many ways. In these final days, though, he spoke to us through a Son. God made his Son the heir of everything and created the world through him.*
>
> *(Hebrews 1:1-2)*

Special Preparation

- Prepare the room with seating arranged in a circle so that everyone will be able to see each other.
- Create a small worship space in the center of the circle with visual reminders of God's presence. For this session that could include an open Bible.
- Have available paper, pens, pencils, and other drawing materials.
- Watch the video segment for Session 3 prior to the session. Prepare a question or two to be used for discussion. Make sure you have a means to show the video to the group.
- Bring a Bible that has special meaning for you and be prepared to talk about why it is important to you.
- Post a large sheet of paper in a visible location in your meeting space. Write the word "Authority" at the top of the sheet.
- Post another large sheet of blank paper for the exercise titled "Explore the Key Questions by Looking for Insights in Scripture."

Getting Started

Opening Activity

Share Bible Stories

If you used the closing activity in the last session that invited participants to bring a Bible with special meaning, allow some time for volunteers to share their stories about why that Bible has special meaning to them. Begin by sharing a Bible of your own and your story of why it is important to you. If there are others who did not bring a Bible, invite them to share stories as well.

Ask the group:

- *Where do you keep your Bible? Do you treat it differently from other books?*
- *What family traditions taught you about how to view the Bible?*

Now invite the group into a contest to find passages that were used in chapter 3 of the study book. Assure them that it is just for fun. Tell the participants that you will call out the passage and they should look it up as quickly as possible. The first one to the passage should raise her or his hand and read the passage aloud. The passages are:

- Hebrews 1:1-2
- John 17:23
- Ephesians 4:4
- 1 Corinthians 2:2

Opening Prayer

Read the following prayer aloud, or use one of your own:

O Living Word,
We love to hear the stories that tell us who we are in your eyes.
We long to know your will and your way as we serve you.
When we find ourselves divided
    by different interpretations and nagging questions,
    send your Spirit to light the path
    and nurture us in a community founded on your grace.
We are eager to meet you here right now.
Come, Lord Jesus, Come. Amen.

Learning Together

Video Study and Discussion

Play the video and ask the group for reactions to it. Ask a question or two that you prepared from viewing the video before the session.

Book and Bible Study and Discussion

Discuss Authority

Say to the group:

- *Chapter 3 of the study book deals with the question of where authority comes from within the revolutionary Christian community formed by Jesus' proclamation of the kingdom of God. Let's start by thinking about how we generally view authority.*

Draw attention to the large sheet of paper you posted before the session began that is titled "Authority." Write responses to the following question on the sheet.

Ask:

• *Who has authority in our community and our society?* (Help group members consider the different forms of authority that people have, including themselves. Possible answers could include government officials, police officers, teachers, parents, and health professionals.)

Ask:

• *How do we relate to the authority of these people? Why is important that we have people with special authority? When does authority become a problem?*

Review the History of Renewal Through Biblical Authority

Divide into three small groups. Assign each of the groups one of the following figures discussed in the opening of chapter 3 of the study book:

• Martin Luther
• John Wesley
• Rutilio Grande

Say:

• *The Bible has often been central to renewal in the Christian church. Mike Slaughter begins chapter 3 by talking about three Christian leaders who found the inspiration for their mission in the Bible. Read the paragraph (or paragraphs) of the chapter that relate to your assigned leader. Then answer these questions:*

1. *What effect did the Bible have on the mission of this leader?*
2. *How did this leader view the Bible?*

Give the small groups some time to work, then come back together as a large group. Give each of the groups time to introduce its assigned figure and the answers to the questions. Ask:

• *When have you been inspired by the Bible to do something new? What kind of authority would you say the Bible had for you?*

Study Scripture Together

Instruct group members to find John 8:2-11 in their Bibles. Have a volunteer read the passage aloud while everyone else follows along. Ask:

- *What happens in this story? Who are the main characters?*

Invite the participants to imagine themselves as the religious leaders who confronted the woman in the story. What authorized their position? How did they make their case?

Now have them imagine themselves as Jesus. Where does he look for authority? What is the new picture he offers of God?

Finally have the group explore the story from the woman's perspective. What does God look like as represented by the men who want to stone her? What does God look like as represented by Jesus?

Read the paragraphs in chapter 3 of the study book that relate to this story. Ask:

- *How do rigid interpretations of Scripture do harm? What are some areas where Christians disagree on their interpretations of the Bible? How do these disagreements lead to division?*

Consider the Model of Francis of Assisi

Ask a participant to read aloud the section of chapter 3 in the study book that relates to Francis of Assisi. Say to the group:

- *We often think of St. Francis as the gentle figure who blessed animals, but Mike Slaughter reminds us that he was also a controversial figure in the Catholic Church of his day.*

Ask:

- *What made Francis controversial? How did Pope Innocent III address the differences between Francis's view of the atonement and the majority of the church? How did this accommodation allow for unity?*

Debate "Agreeing to Disagree"

Separate the group into two smaller groups.

Say:

- *Mike Slaughter writes in his book about Phyllis Tickle's belief that the Christian church is going through a major revolutionary shift that can bring Kingdom renewal. One of Mike's concerns is how the church maintains its unity when there is so much disagreement over biblical interpretation. Let's explore what options there are for us to "agree to disagree."*

Assign each group one of the following positions, recognizing that some people may be arguing for a position that they do not hold:

1. When there is a major disagreement on a matter of biblical interpretation, it is better for the church to split.
2. When there is a major disagreement on a matter of biblical interpretation, it is important to maintain our unity.

Have each group build a case for the position they have been assigned.

- What biblical passages or stories help support this position?
- What are the implications of this position for the church?

After allowing some time for small group work, have the groups share their position with the other group listening respectfully while one presents. After both sides have presented, allow time for respectful questions of each side. Thank both groups for their work and then gather as a whole group.

Read aloud Ephesians 4:3-6. Ask:

- *What does this passage suggest about the basis for Christian unity? How can this passage help us when we confront our disagreements?*

Explore the Key Questions by Looking for Insights in Scripture

In the section of chapter 3 titled "The Key Questions," Mike Slaughter begins by talking about three questions that we have about the authority of the Bible. Begin by reading those three questions aloud. Then say:

- *Mike Slaughter says that there are several insights on those questions that are given by Scripture itself. Let's see if we can find at least three in the paragraphs that follow where he talks about Jesus' interactions with religious leaders at the pool of Bethesda.*

Invite participants to scan these paragraphs silently for a few minutes. Then ask them to call out insights from the paragraphs about biblical authority. Write responses on a large sheet of paper you posted before the session began. Make sure that you note at least these three:

1. Our picture of God will impact our interpretation of Scripture.
2. The New Testament community had a new picture of God that impacted their relationships with God and each other.
3. The early church also had a new revolutionary authority—Jesus, the Living Word.

Ask:

- *How did the authority of Jesus relate to the authority of the Scriptures? What does it mean that God has spoken through Jesus? Why does Mike Slaughter say that Jesus didn't leave us with a book but with a living presence?*

Draw a Picture of the One Absolute

Distribute pieces of paper and drawing instruments to participants. Say to the group:

- *Mike Slaughter reminds us of Paul's statement of the one absolute that holds Christians together. It is written in 1 Corinthians 2:2. Look up that passage and write it at the bottom of the piece of paper you just received. Then draw a picture in whatever style you like of what that source of Christian unity is.*

Allow group members time to work on their drawings. Then come back together as a larger group and invite volunteers to share their drawings and what it means to them. Ask:

- *How would you use this drawing to explain to someone who is unfamiliar with the Christian faith what that faith is all about? What do you believe Mike Slaughter means when he says, "Our stance* is Jesus. Everything else is a conversation!"*? How does seeing the crucified Christ as our one absolute help us put the Bible in proper perspective?*

Wrapping Up

Closing Activity

Create a Reminder of Christian Unity

Ask participants to hold the picture they have just created in their hands and to look at it silently. Say:

- *In this session we have talked about how the words of the Bible have been an inspiration for renewal in every period of the church's history. We also have talked about how Christ and the continuing presence and guidance of the Holy Spirit help us understand God's will in new and changing times. Think about a place in your home where you could place this picture. Perhaps by the mirror in your bathroom or in the closet where you get your clothes each day. Think about how it might remind you of the importance of Christ's work and of Christ's desire that the church might be united. Take this home and put it in that place between now and the next session.*

Closing Prayer

Offer the following prayer or one of your own:

Christ, the Living Word,
We call upon your Spirit to look beyond our rigid expectations
*   to the new breath you desire to breathe upon this land.*
Make us faithful in our response to your promise
*   to give us what we need to resist the evil forces that oppress*
and let your kingdom come, your will be done. Amen.

Session 4

KINGDOM POLITICS

Planning the Session

Session Goals

As a result of conversations and activities connected with this session, group members should begin to

- understand the alternative definition of power in the kingdom of God as one in which weakness can be strength;
- consider the Beatitudes in Matthew 5:1-12 as an explication of the upside-down politics of the kingdom of God;
- explore how the values on display in the Beatitudes address problems in our lives and world today;
- commit to living out a life of righteousness and mercy even if it involves persecution.

Scriptural Foundation

> *[God] said to me, "My grace is enough for you, because power is made perfect in weakness." So I'll gladly spend my time bragging about my weaknesses so that Christ's power can rest on me. Therefore, I'm all right with weaknesses, insults, disasters, harassments, and stressful situations for the sake of Christ, because when I'm weak, then I'm strong.*
>
> *(2 Corinthians 12:9-10)*

37

Special Preparation

- Prepare the room with seating arranged in a circle so that everyone will be able to see each other.
- Create a small worship space in the center of the circle with visual reminders of God's presence. For this session that could include a candle and a basin and towel.
- Have available scissors, paper, pens, pencils, and other drawing materials.
- Also have available Bibles for those who may not have brought one.
- Watch the video segment for Session 4 prior to the session. Prepare a question or two to be used for discussion. Make sure you have a means to show the video to the group.
- Collect newspapers and magazines that cover current events and culture. Make sure you're not too attached to them since you will invite participants to cut them up. Have them available for the exercise titled "Define Power in the Kingdom of God."
- Post two large, blank sheets of paper in a visible location for the exercise titled "Define Power in the Kingdom of God."
- Prepare a large sheet of paper with the title "Beatitudes Match-Up 1." Write the following incomplete sentences on it in this order. (Verses are from the NRSV.) Then post the paper in a visible and accessible spot in your meeting space:
  o Blessed are the poor in spirit . . .
  o Blessed are those who mourn . . .
  o Blessed are the meek . . .
  o Blessed are those who hunger and thirst for righteousness . . .
  o Blessed are the merciful . . .
  o Blessed are the pure in heart . . .
  o Blessed are the peacemakers . . .
  o Blessed are those who are persecuted for righteousness' sake . . .
- Prepare a large sheet of paper with the title "Beatitudes Match-Up 2." Write the following incomplete sentences on it in this order. Then post the paper in a visible and accessible spot in your meeting space:

o ... for they will see God.

o ... for they will be called children of God.

o ... for theirs is the kingdom of heaven.

o ... for they will be receive mercy.

o ... for they will be comforted.

o ... for they will inherit the earth.

o ... for theirs is the kingdom of heaven.

o ... for they will be filled.

- Have available sticky notes, preferably of different colors, for the exercise titled "Consider the Beatitudes."

Getting Started

Opening Activity

Reflect on the Prodigal Son

Ask group members to turn in their Bible to Luke 15:14-19. Say:

- *We're going to begin this session with some reflection on the story that Jesus tells about a father and two sons, often called the parable of the prodigal son. We're going to pick up the story with the younger son living in a far country and coming to an important realization about himself. But before we do, let's remind ourselves what's happened to get him to this point.*

Invite the group to share, from memory, the story as told in Luke 15:11-13. If persons are unfamiliar with the story, you can have them scan these verses to respond. Now ask a participant to read verses 14-19.

Have the group members reflect silently on the following questions. Pause between each question to allow for brief reflection:

- *What was it that the younger son realized about himself?*
- *How did he decide to respond?*
- *When have you had to come to a difficult realization about yourself?*
- *How did you respond?*

Now ask another reader to read aloud Luke 15:20-24.

Again ask the group members to reflect silently on the following questions:

- *How did the father respond to his returning son?*
- *What was the basis for the father's actions?*
- *When has someone received you in such a way that you realized your worth was not in what you had done but who you were in their eyes?*

Opening Prayer

Read the following prayer aloud, or use one of your own:

God who welcomes home the broken,
We have a hard time not being in control.
We get confused about what constitutes power
*   and the source of our own worth.*
We want to lay aside the things
*   that keep us from drawing closer to you.*
We want to know our home in you. Amen.

Learning Together

Video Study and Discussion

Play the video and ask the group for reactions to it. Ask a question or two that you prepared from viewing the video before the session.

Book and Bible Study and Discussion

Define Power in the Kingdom of God

Distribute the newspapers and magazines that you collected prior to the session. Have scissors available. Say to the group:

- *In chapter 4 Mike Slaughter talks about top ten lists of the world's most powerful people. He says that the criteria those lists used seemed to be: "how many people they had power or influence over, the financial resources they controlled, if they had power across multiple spheres, and how actively they used their power to change the world."*

Using those criteria, see how many powerful people you can find in these publications. Cut out articles or pictures with people you would nominate for our top ten list.

Give participants time to look through the newspapers and magazines and to cut out articles and pictures. Then convene the whole group and have volunteers share their nominees for the top ten. Place the cut-out contributions on a table or the floor, or post them on a wall. After all the nominations are made, come up with a group ranking of the top ten. (Discourage extensive discussion. This should be a brief exercise.) Ask:

• *What makes these people powerful? If we were to define power based on the qualities these people have, what would it be?*

Write responses to these questions on a blank sheet of paper you have posted in a visible location. Now ask:

• *What makes the power Jesus embodied different? What are the qualities that make for power in the kingdom of God?*

Write responses to these questions on another blank sheet of paper. Have a volunteer read aloud 2 Corinthians 12:9-10. Ask:

• *How would does Paul define power in the kingdom of God?*

Use the responses to this question to write a definition of power on the second sheet of paper. Ask:

• *If we took this definition of power seriously, what would change about how we live in the world?*

Consider the Beatitudes
For the next exercise, ask group members to keep their Bibles and study books closed. Say:

• *Mike Slaughter says that the "upside-down 'foolishness' of revolutionary kingdom politics" is very evident in the Beatitudes, a part of Jesus' Sermon on the Mount as found in Matthew 5. Let's see how much we remember about this famous passage of scripture.*

Have participants find a partner. Give each pair a set of sticky notes, preferably of different colors. Ask the pairs, without looking at Bibles or study books, to write down the incomplete sentences that are written on the sheet you prepared earlier titled "Beatitudes Match-Up 2"—one incomplete sentence to each sticky note.

Now have the pair place each sticky note by one of the incomplete sentences on the sheet you prepared earlier titled "Beatitudes Match-Up 1." The resulting complete sentence should be one of Jesus' Beatitudes from Matthew 5.

After everyone has placed all of their sticky notes, read together Matthew 5:1-12. Note how many correct responses there were. Now ask:

- *What would the people called "blessed" in the Beatitudes actually be called by most people in the world? What does this list suggest about the way God views what is powerful? What makes these qualities difficult for us?*

Discuss the Power of Shame

Say to the group:

- *Mike Slaughter says that the conditions referred to in the Beatitudes reflect problems that relate to the brokenness of our lives and of the world. In the section of chapter 4 where he talks about "those who mourn," Mike addresses the issue of shame and how it distorts us.*

Invite the group to skim the section of chapter 4 titled "Blessed Are Those Who Mourn."

Now move through the section by asking the following questions:

- *How does Mike restate the beatitude on mourning in the first paragraph?*
- *What is the pain that he says we share?*

Say to the group:

- *Mike shares his feelings about his upcoming high school reunion and the painful memories of his childhood that reunions can trigger.*

Ask:

- *What feelings come up for you when you think about going to a reunion? What makes it difficult to revisit vulnerable periods in our lives? According to Mike, how does our own pain sometimes lead us to shaming others?*

Say to the group:

- *Mike talks about social media and politics as areas where public shaming has been especially prevalent in recent years.*

Ask:

- *What is the cost of being vulnerable in public spaces like social media? What considerations are in your mind when you think about posting on social media platforms?*

Say to the group:

- *Mike concludes this section by talking about Christ's "amazing grace" as God's response to the brokenness in our lives.*

Ask:

- *Where have you seen Christ's grace in your life? in the world? How does that grace transform situations where we are tempted to "blame and shame" others?*

Explore Our Commitment to Righteousness and Mercy

Distribute paper and writing utensils to participants. Ask them to make an activity diary of the last full weekday before this session. Assure them that they will not be asked to share this diary with anyone. Have the group members begin by listing the approximate time when they woke up on that day. Then list, in rough detail, all the things they did during the day with their estimates of how much time they spent doing those activities.

Now review the section of chapter 4 titled "Blessed Are Those Who Hunger and Thirst for Righteousness." Read the section aloud or have a volunteer read it. Ask:

- *How does Mike Slaughter describe righteousness? How is seeking a right relationship with God different from seeking fulfillment from other sources?*

Invite the group members to turn again to their diaries and review them. Ask:

- *How much time did you spend on taking care of personal and family needs? on work? Where are there times when you were engaged in activities that helped you grow in your pursuit of righteousness?*

Turn again to chapter 4 and read the section titled "Blessed Are the Merciful." Ask:

- *What is mercy, according to Mike Slaughter? How is it revealed? Why is it important that mercy be paired with righteousness?*

Review your diaries once again. Ask:

- *How much time did you spend on acts of mercy during the day? What are some regular practices that we might engage in that would help us be more mindful of the importance of pursuing righteousness and mercy in our daily lives?*

Say to the group:

- *Mike Slaughter says that we need the community and accountability of other Jesus-followers who are seeking to live out a kingdom-of-God worldview. These Christian friends can give us encouragement as we seek to be open to God's transforming work in us.*

Ask:

- *Where do you find encouragement and accountability? What makes it difficult to find Christian community in which you can be open and vulnerable? How might such a community strengthen your personal practices of discipleship?*

Invite group members to spend a few minutes looking at their diary again and sketching out how they might organize their activities for tomorrow. How could they make some intentional time to grow closer to God? Is there a person or organization that needs help they could offer? Write out a plan for the day. Then ask the participants to write down the names of two or three people who they believe could help them stay accountable to this journey. Invite group members to call and talk with these people this week and discuss ways they could deepen their relationship as Christian friends.

When everyone has had a chance to do some reflecting and writing, invite volunteers to share any ideas or learnings they had during the exercise.

Wrapping Up

Closing Activity

Explore the Idea of Persecution as Privilege

Invite group members to review silently the section of chapter 4 titled "Blessed Are the Persecuted." Say to the group:

- *Mike Slaughter says that everyone who commits to following Jesus should expect resistance and even persecution. He also says that persecution is a privilege.*

Ask:

- *According to Mike, what are three ways that persecution is a privilege?* [Answers should include: 1) it opens the eyes of others, 2) it drives us to prayer and praise, and 3) it teaches us the Kingdom value of perseverance.]

Invite group members to consider how they have seen persecution in the lives of other Christians strengthen their own faith.

Closing Prayer

Read the following prayer aloud, or use one of your own:

God, you call us to live in a Kingdom with upside-down values
when considered from the perspective of this world.
We want to follow where you lead
despite our fears.
We want to follow where you lead
because you are our hope. Amen.

Session 5

KINGDOM ECONOMY

Planning the Session

Session Goals

As a result of conversations and activities connected with this session, group members should begin to

- explore the difference between earthly economics built on a strategy of scarcity and a Kingdom economy founded on an assumption of abundance;
- consider the implications of the affirmation that all things belong to God;
- examine ways that we can be involved in caring for creation in an era of changing climate;
- understand the long-term impacts of economic inequality and how we can be engaged in addressing them.

Scriptural Foundation

> *The earth is the LORD's and everything in it,*
> *the world and its inhabitants too.*
>
> *(Psalm 24:1)*

Special Preparation

- Prepare the room with seating arranged in a circle so that everyone will be able to see each other.
- Create a small worship space in the center of the circle with visual reminders of God's presence.
- Have available paper, pens, pencils, and other drawing materials.
- Also have available Bibles for those who may not have brought one.
- Watch the video segment for Session 5 prior to the session. Prepare a question or two to be used for discussion. Make sure you have a means to show the video to the group.
- Prepare bags for the opening activity. Get enough small brown paper bags for every member of the group. Also obtain small pieces of individually wrapped candies. You will need enough individual pieces for the following distribution:
  - o 35 pieces for 1 bag
  - o 10 pieces for 3 bags
  - o 2 pieces for 3 bags
  - o 1 piece for the remaining bags
  Close each bag and staple the top together.
- Have two pieces of posterboard for the exercise titled "Study Scripture Together."
- Post a large sheet of paper in a visible spot in your meeting space.
- Write the title "Doing Our Part on Climate Change" across the top of another large sheet of paper. Post this sheet in a visible spot as well.

Getting Started

Opening Activity

Do an Exercise on Abundance and Scarcity

As participants enter the room, hand them, at random, one of the small paper bags you prepared before the session. Tell the participants not to open the bag before you tell them to do so.

After everyone has arrived, say to the group:

- *It seems that we never have enough—enough time, enough resources, enough money. It also seems that what we do have is not fairly distributed. Let's do an exercise to see if there is another way to look at things.*
- *Each of you has a bag. The good news is that it has candy in it. The bad news is that you may not have very much candy. Let's pretend that the candy represents wealth and that it takes one piece of candy to survive per year.*

Now invite group members to open their bags. Ask:

- *What do you notice about your wealth? What do you notice about your neighbor's wealth? What are some possible explanations for why there is a disparity in the wealth in each bag?* (Possible answers include: Some people are more favored. It was luck. We got what we earned.)

Say:

- *Now imagine that there is a refugee crisis in your country. There are thirty people coming to your community who have no resources and will need help for a year. Remember you need one piece of candy to survive for a year.*

Ask:

- *Do we have enough wealth to take care of 30 people? How will we respond to this crisis? How does our individual situation affect our sense of scarcity or abundance?*

Opening Prayer

Read the following prayer aloud, or use one of your own:

God of all creation,
*   You have provided us with abundance*
*   But there are those among us who live in scarcity.*

Our economics don't reflect your gracious excess.
Help us see what you see.
In Jesus' name. Amen.

Learning Together

Video Study and Discussion

Play the video and ask the group for reactions to it. Ask a question or two that you prepared from viewing the video before the session.

Book and Bible Study and Discussion

Study Scripture Together

Say to the group:

- *In the opening section of chapter 5 in the study book, Mike Slaughter talks about the "scarcity mentality" that characterizes how the world thinks about resources.*

Ask:

- *What do you think Mike means by a "scarcity mentality"? How have you seen this mentality at work in the world? in the church? in your life?*

Say:

- *In contrast to the scarcity mentality, God's kingdom talks about abundance. Let's look at two of the passages Mike lifts up to see how the Bible talks about Kingdom abundance.*

Divide into two small groups. Provide each group with a piece of posterboard and some drawing instruments. Assign one of the following two passages to each group:

- Malachi 3:10
- Luke 6:38

Ask them to read their assigned passage aloud and then consider the following questions:

- *What is the basic message of this passage?*
- *Where have you seen people living out this belief?*
- *What does this passage say about God?*

After allowing some time for discussion, ask each small group to paraphrase the passage (put it in their own words) or to choose a phrase from the verse that captures the main idea. Design and color a poster with those words that you will then post on the wall.

When the groups come back together, have them present their poster along with any insights from their small group discussion.

Explore the Implications of Stewardship

Ask group members to turn to the opening section of chapter 5 in the study book. Say to the group:

- *At the end of the first section of this chapter, Mike Slaughter says that there are two Kingdom economic principles that often contrast sharply with the way we think about economics.*

Ask:

- *What are these two Kingdom economic principles?*

Write responses on a large sheet of paper that you posted before the session began. [The two principles are: 1) Everything belongs to God, and 2) God's kingdom design calls for economic justice.] Now say to the group:

- *In the next section of chapter 5, Mike talks about the first of these principles—"It All Belongs to God." Skim over this section and identify the three biblical passages that help illuminate this principle.*

Ask:

- *What are the three passages? What does each passage tell us about the implications of the truth that everything belongs to God? If we* took these passages seriously, what would change about the way we think about and use the resources God has made available to us?

Make Plans to Do Our Part

Say to the group:

- *In the section of chapter 5 titled "The Earth Matters," Mike Slaughter quotes numerous Bible passages related to God's care and concern for the earth and our responsibility for it.*

Have group members skim through the section and read aloud Bible passages that they find. Ask:

- *What do these verses say about God's role as Creator? about the value of the creation in God's eyes? about our role as stewards of creation?*

Now have the group look at the section titled "Doing Our Part." Say to the group:

- *This section includes eight different suggestions for what we can do individually to help address climate change. Let's consider each one and what it would mean for our lives if we adopted them.*

Read each of the suggestions in this section. Write them on the large sheet of paper you posted before the session titled "Doing Our Part on Climate Change." After each suggestion, ask:

- *How would this change affect my current lifestyle? What are some steps I could take to live into this change?*

After all eight of the suggestions are on the sheet, invite group members to reflect silently on what new practice they would be willing to undertake to move toward one of these goals. Have group members write down one new practice on a piece of paper. Encourage them to take this paper with them and to put in a place where they will see it during the week. Invite volunteers to share their commitment.

Now ask the group to consider larger-scale changes to address climate change. Ask:

- *Why is it difficult for us to address climate change on a planetary scale? How does a kingdom-of-God perspective differ from the perspective taken by political parties?*

Take a Look at the Numbers on Wealth Inequality

Say to the group:

- *Now let's look at the other principle of Kingdom economics— economic justice. In the section of chapter 5 titled "The Problem of Wealth Inequality," Mike Slaughter shares a number of statistics that illustrate economic inequity.*

Ask the group to scan the section titled "The Problem of Wealth Inequality" looking for statistics. When someone finds a statistic, ask her or him to read it out loud. Ask:

- *What economic problem does this statistic point to? What sort of injustice is this? What would this statistic look like if we were living by Kingdom economics?*

Then say:

- *Mike also talks about some of the consequences of inequality and economic injustice.*

Ask:

- *According to the study book, what are some of the physical effects of inequality? Where do you see economic inequality in your community? What organizations are helping address these inequities?*

Consider How You Can Help One Life at a Time

Say to the group:

- *In the final section of chapter 5, Mike tells the story of Shannon and how his church came alongside her to help change her situation.*

Invite group members to skim the section of chapter 5 titled "One Life at a Time." Ask:

- *What were the particular challenges that Shannon faced? What changes on the political level could help her situation? What did the church do to intercede on her behalf?*

Now invite participants to silently reflect on someone they know who is undergoing a difficult time financially. What is this person or family going through? What sort of help would address their situation?

Have everyone find a partner for the next exercise. Ask the pairs to decide which of them will be the speaker first and which will be the listener. Now ask the speaker to describe the person they have been reflecting on without naming them. Give the speaker sixty seconds to describe the person. Now allow the listener in the pair to ask the speaker clarifying questions. Then have the pairs brainstorm about resources in your church or community that could help this situation.

After allowing some time for discussion, switch and have the person in each pair who was listening become the speaker. Give them sixty seconds to describe the person they have been imagining. Then allow for clarifying questions from the listening partner and some time for brainstorming.

Close this exercise by asking each pair to pray for the persons they have been discussing. Ask them also to commit for praying for these persons during the upcoming week.

Wrapping Up

Closing Activity

Imagine Responsibility and Stewardship

As you close, invite group members to engage in an exercise of active imagination with you. Ask them to close their eyes and to cup their hands facing upward in an open position on their lap. Now ask them to imagine all the things and people for which they are responsible sitting in the bowl formed by the palms of their hands. Ask:

- *What and who are you responsible for? Are there pets? children? aging relatives? cars? houses? community organizations?*

Now invite participants to raise their hands up as you pray the closing prayer.

Closing Prayer

God who made us,
   these things we hold in our hands can be heavy.
Sometimes we wonder if the burden is too much.
And sometimes we are forgetful
   and less faithful stewards than we want to be.
Help us to give these things,
   which you made, back to you
and trust that you provide all that we need to bear our responsibilities.
Give us this day our daily bread. Amen.

Invite group members to separate their hands and raise them up to God as a closing act of trust.

Session 6
THE "ALL IN"

Planning the Session

Session Goals

As a result of conversations and activities connected with this session, group members should begin to

- understand how the narrative of the Christian story, including the vision of God's kingdom, emphasizes the importance of faith over fear;
- explore the dangers of moral relativism and political expediency, particularly as they harm the church's mission to younger generations;
- consider how Christians are called to engage in God's work of combating racism and xenophobia in order to embody a Kingdom of all races;
- examine the ways in which God's tearing down walls of hostility opens up the possibility of ministry between generations and using the gifts of women and LGBTQ persons.

Scriptural Foundation

> *Christ is our peace. He made both Jews and Gentiles into one group. With his body, he broke down the barrier of hatred that*

> *divided us. He canceled the detailed rules of the Law so that he could create one new person out of the two groups, making peace. He reconciled them both as one body to God by the cross, which ended the hostility to God.*
>
> (Ephesians 2:14-16)

Special Preparation

- Prepare the room with seating arranged in a circle so that everyone will be able to see each other.
- Create a small worship space in the center of the circle with visual reminders of God's presence.
- Have available paper, pens, pencils, and other drawing materials.
- Also have available Bibles for those who may not have brought one.
- Post three large sheets of blank paper in a visible and accessible location in your meeting space.
- Purchase some simple thank-you cards with plenty of blank space or make some of your own for the exercise titled "Consider Support for Female Leaders."

Getting Started

Opening Activity

Envision the Restored Creation

Invite group members to open their Bibles to Revelation 7:9-17. Say to the group:

- *In chapter 6 of the study book, Mike Slaughter talks about what we find at "the end of the book." Revelation is the last book in the Bible, and it gives us a picture of what God's future looks like. In this passage the writer, John, gives us a vision of that scene.*

Ask a volunteer reader to read the passage aloud. Now invite group members to read the passage again silently, noting the visual images.

Direct attention to one of the large sheets of blank paper you posted before the session began. Tell the group that you are going to collaborate to create a picture of this scene from Revelation 7. Invite volunteers to come up, one at a time, to draw an element of the scene and to point out where that element is mentioned in the Bible passage. You can begin by drawing the throne and the lamb from verse 9 in the center of the sheet. Emphasize to group members that they will not be judged on the quality of their drawing. Stick figures are OK!

Continue until you have included as many of the visual elements as possible. Then ask:

- *What is comforting about this image? What is challenging? What is the importance of the fact that people of every nation are represented?*

Opening Prayer

Read the following prayer or offer one of your own:

Lamb of God, we long to see what John saw—
*   all people gathered in worship before your throne.*
We know the walls that divide us
*   and we sometimes despair that they will ever come down.*
But we give thanks for the future you have revealed
And we lean toward it in your reconciling power. Amen.

Learning Together

Video Study and Discussion

Play the video and ask the group for reactions to it. Ask a question or two that you prepared from viewing the video before the session.

Book and Bible Study and Discussion

Study Scripture Together

Ask group members to find Ephesians 2:14-16 in their Bibles. Say to the group:

- *The Book of Ephesians gives us a powerful image of how Christ breaks down walls between people who have been divided—in this case Jews and Gentiles (non-Jews) who were both finding their way into the new Christian community. Let's read a passage that is at the heart of Ephesians' message.*

Have someone read aloud Ephesians 2:14-16. Ask:

- *What does this passage say about Christ? What does Christ do? What is the result of Christ's work?*

Invite the group to reflect on the central message of this biblical passage. Ask:

How would we write the central message in our own words?

On another sheet of blank paper that you posted before the session, write a group summary of the response to this question.

Now invite the participants to name people and groups who are divided by barriers of hatred in our world today. Write responses on the paper below the summary.

Have the group turn to the opening paragraphs of chapter 6 in the study book where Mike Slaughter addresses the barriers that divide us from one another. Read these paragraphs aloud. Then ask:

- *What is Mike's answer to the question of why we keep rebuilding the walls that Christ came to tear down? What feeds our division? How does the vision of Christ's revolutionary kingdom confront the ways we are divided?*

After allowing some time for discussion of these questions, close this exercise by having the group read aloud Ephesians 2:14-16 once again. (If your group members are using multiple translations, you may need to have this read aloud by a single voice.)

Role-play a Discussion Between Younger and Older Generations

Invite group members to skim the section of chapter 6 titled "Evangelical Relativism." Say to the group:

- *In this section, Mike Slaughter talks about how younger generations are viewing the church in the current political environment.*

Ask:

- *How has the view of evangelicals changed during Mike's lifetime? What are some of the factors that cause young adults to either opt out of church or to avoid it altogether? What statistics does Mike cite that tell how younger generations relate to church?*

Now divide into two groups. Have one group explore the religious landscape of Americans as if they are boomers or older (55 and up) while the other group assumes the perspective of young millennials (born 1990–96) and how they view the church and the world. Give each group a piece of paper and ask them to list responses to the following questions (you may need to write these on a large piece of paper or have copies available):

- *What life stage were you in when these major national events happened?*
  - o the 2001 attacks on the World Trade Center and Pentagon
  - o the revelations of sexual abuse in the Catholic Church (circa 2004)
  - o the financial crisis of 2008
  - o the legalization of same-sex marriage nationwide by the Supreme Court in 2015
- *How did they affect your view of the church and the world?*
- *What role does the church play in your life?*
- *What might be difficult to understand about older Christians* (if you are a millennial) *or younger people* (if you are a boomer or older)?

Acknowledge to the group that there is no one profile that fits all older or younger people and that each age group encompasses a lot of diversity.

Allow some time for small group work; then ask each group to choose one person who will role-play a member of their age group in a conversation. Encourage the person chosen to use their imagination to fill out the character. Then have the two representatives come to sit in front of the whole group. Pretend that you are the interviewer facilitating the conversation. Ask the questions that the small groups worked on. Then ask:

- *What would you like the other person in this conversation to know about your experience? What does Jesus look like for you?*

Thank the volunteers for their willingness to do the role-play. Then ask the whole group:

- *How can we foster conversations like this between generations?*

Discuss the Fort McKinley Example

Invite the group to turn in chapter 6 in the study book to the section titled "A Kingdom of All Races." Say:

- *Racism is one of the ways that we still experience the walls of division. In this section of the study book, Mike Slaughter talks about how, even after milestones like school desegregation and the Civil Rights Act, we still have a long way to go. As one way to address this, Mike encourages Christians to work harder at desegregating themselves. He uses the example of the Fort McKinley Campus of his Ginghamsburg Church to illustrate this.*

Read aloud the paragraphs that discuss the relationship between Ginghamsburg's Tipp City and Fort McKinley campuses. Ask:

- *What does Mike like about the Fort McKinley Campus? What challenges emerged between the Fort McKinley and Tipp City campuses? What did Mike and the Tipp City Campus learn as a result of these challenges?*

Now consider your own community of faith. Ask:

- *How does our congregation or community of faith reflect the community we live in? If we wanted to become more racially and economically diverse, what would need to change? How can we expand our social networks outside the church to be more racially diverse?*

Design a Campaign on Immigration

In the same section of chapter 6, Mike Slaughter addresses the current debate about immigration. He shares a conversation he had with Katie Kersh, an immigration attorney and advocate. Read aloud the paragraphs in which Katie identifies three big fallacies that Americans have about immigrants.

Write the responses to the following question on a large sheet of paper that you posted before the session began. Ask:

- *What are the three fallacies about immigrants that Katie Kersh names?* [1) immigrants are dangerous, 2) immigrants are stealing American jobs, and 3) immigrants are a threat to American lives, language, and religion.]

Now invite group members to design a campaign that would offer a more accurate picture of immigrants. Ask:

- *What information does Katie give that counters these fallacies?*

Read Exodus 22:21 and Deuteronomy 10:19 from the Bible. Ask:

- *What do these verses suggest about the way God views immigrants and the way that God's people should treat them? How could we express this in an informational campaign at our church?*

Distribute paper and drawing materials and allow participants, individually or in small groups, to sketch a poster that could be used as part of the campaign. Invite volunteers to share their work with the group.

Consider Support for Female Leaders

Invite group members to scan the section of chapter 6 titled "A Gender-Inclusive Kingdom." Ask a volunteer to summarize the response that a Facebook post of the Rev. Rachel Billups received. Ask:

- *How did the church respond to the negative post? What are the biblical examples of female leadership that Mike lifts up? What other biblical models of female leadership can you think of?*

Now list the names of female leaders, clergy and laity, in your community of faith or in the larger community. Ask:

- *What message could we share with these women that shows that their leadership is valued and respected?*

Distribute the thank-you cards that you purchased or made before the session began. Invite participants to take a card and write a message to one of the women they have identified. Ask the group members to give or mail the card to its intended recipient in the coming week.

Wrapping Up

Closing Activity

Name the Walls That Need to Come Down
Ask group members to reflect on all of the walls that are mentioned in chapter 6 of the study book. Have them name those walls aloud. You can add any that do not get mentioned. The walls should include the following: between generations, racism, xenophobia, sexism, heterosexism, and ageism.

Now direct attention to the picture of the Kingdom you created in the opening exercise. Ask group members to imagine all of the people who are included in God's grace.

Closing Prayer

Ask group members to form a circle and hold hands. Since this is the last session, thank the participants for their willingness to discuss difficult issues and for their respect for one another.

Invite volunteers to share a gift they received through participation in the class. You should begin this exercise to model this.

Close the session by praying together the Lord's Prayer.